OUR
AMERICA

GROWING UP
IN THE
GREAT
DEPRESSION

1929
TO
1941

AMY RUTH

Lerner Publications Company
Minneapolis

The author gratefully acknowledges the following individuals whose stories are told, in part, throughout the pages of this book: Ann Marie Low, Blink, Bob and Dorothy Simonson, Clancy Strock, Clarence Lee, Don Blincoe, Inez Williamson, Jeems, Joe Montgomery, Loraine Johnson, Lucille Boyette, the Tathem and Turner families, Tom, and Toni Johnson. Thanks also must go to editor Sara Saetre, whose insight, vision and thoughtful prodding contributed significantly to the making of this book.

Lerner Publications
A division of Lerner Publishing Group
241 First Avenue North
Minneapolis, MN 55401 U.S.A.

Website address: www.lernerbooks.com

Photographs and illustrations in this book are used courtesy of: Franklin D. Roosevelt Library, pp. 5 [48223704 (427) C], 12 (NLR-PHOCO-A-7182), 14 (71-80), 20 (58381), 30; © Bettmann/CORBIS, pp. 6, 9, 10; Library of Congress, pp. 7 (LC-USF34-02086-E), 15 (LC-USF33-000553-M4), 16 (LC-USF34-008660-D), 17 (LC-USF34-044526-D), 18 (LC-USF33-030239-M1), 21 top (LC-USF34-071887-D), 21 bottom (LC-USZC2-987), 22 (LC-USZ62-11491), 23 (LC-USF34-004047-E), 24 (LC-USF33-12312-MI), 26 (LC-USF34-009986-C), 27 (LC-USF33-013161-M2), 28 (LC-USF33-003497-M1), 29 (LC-USF34-030782-D), 32 (LC-USF34-061343-D), 35 left (LC-USZC2-5552), 35 right (LC-USZC2-5573), 36 (LC-USF34-008596-D), 53 (LC-USZC2-862); National Archives, pp. 13 (NWDNS-119-CAL-7), 41 (NWDNS-119-CAL-108), 52 (NWDNS-35-G-3K-3), 55 (NWDNS-119-CAL-210), 56 (NWDNS-119-CAL-156), 57 (NWDNS-83-G-37944); United States Department of Agriculture, pp. 31 (01di1496), 34 (01di0979), 40 (01di1430); © Sasha/Archive Photos, p. 37; Milwaukee Public Museum, p. 38; Los Angeles Times History Center, p. 39; Minnesota Historical Society, pp. 42, 44, 47; © Todd Strand/Independent Picture Service, p. 43; © CORBIS, p. 46; Batman is a Trademark of DC Comics, © 1939, p. 48; Denver Public Library Western History Department, p 50; © Archive Photos, p. 51; © Underwood & Underwood/CORBIS, p. 54.
Front cover image: United States Department of Agriculture (00di0854)

Library of Congress Cataloging-in-Publication Data

Ruth, Amy.
　　Growing up in the Great Depression, 1929 to 1941 / by Amy Ruth.
　　　p.　cm. — (Our America)
　　Includes bibliographical references and index.
　　Summary: Describes what life was like for young people and their families during the harsh times of the Depression, from 1929 to the beginning of World War II.
　　ISBN 0-8225-0655-6 (lib. bdg. : alk. paper)
　　1. United States—History—1933–1945—Juvenile literature. 2. Depressions—1929—United States—Juvenile literature. 3. United States—Social life and customs—1918–1945—Juvenile literature. 4. United States—History—1933–1945—Sources—Juvenile literature. 5. Children—United States—Social life and customs—20th century—Juvenile literature. 6. Children—United States—Social conditions—20th century—Juvenile literature. [1. Depressions—1929. 2. United States—Social conditions—1918–1932—Sources. 3. United States—Social conditions—1933–1945—Sources.] I. Title. II. Series.
E806 .R88 2003
973.91—dc21   2001006824

Manufactured in the United States of America
1 2 3 4 5 6 – JR – 08 07 06 05 04 03

CONTENTS

NOTE
TO
READERS

Studying history is a way of investigating the mysteries of the past. To gather clues about a past time, historians examine things made during that time. They read old diaries and letters. They look at old newspapers and magazines. They listen to old songs. All these things from the past are called primary sources.

In this book, the author used many primary sources to learn about life in the United States in the 1930s. During this time, known as the Great Depression, everyday life was much different than it is in modern times. Banks and businesses failed, and many Americans lost their savings and their jobs.

Many books about history are historical fiction—made-up stories set

During the depression, people looked up to President
Franklin Delano Roosevelt *(seated)*.

in a real time. But the people you will meet in this book are real.
By looking at their photographs, you'll see what they looked like and
understand how they lived. You'll hear their voices in their letters and
diaries and learn firsthand what they thought and how they felt. Their
words are printed here just the way they were written, misspellings
and all.

In this book, you'll have a chance to explore the past on your own.
You'll glimpse what it was like to live through the hard times of the
1930s. Even though the Great Depression was long ago, your new
ideas about the past can help Americans everywhere build a better
understanding of it.

CHAPTER ONE

THE
CRASH

"This year, Bud and I did it all."

—Ann Marie Low, North Dakota farm girl, 1929

In November 1929, Ann Marie Low remarked in her diary, "There seems to be quite a furor in the country over a big stock market crash that wiped a lot of people out." Ann Marie, a spunky North Dakota farm girl, was referring to October 29, 1929. On that day, sometimes called Black Tuesday, the American stock market dropped in value.

Black Tuesday began a period of hardship known as the Great Depression. Americans were living out a harsh game of survival. Workers lost their jobs, families lost their homes, and some children had to drop out of school.

The depression hit Americans everywhere: in cities, small towns, and farms. On the Low's farm, changes came quickly. "Dad can't afford to hire the help badly needed for farm work," Ann Marie wrote in her journal. "This year, Bud and I did it all." Ann Marie and her brother, Bud, planted the fields, tended the gardens, milked the cows, and did other farm chores. Because Ann Marie was a girl, she also helped her mother and younger sister Ethel clean house, cook, and tend to other household tasks.

Like many Americans, Ann Marie thought the tough times would not last long. "Maybe next year we

Opposite: New Yorkers read news of the stock market crash at the New York Stock Exchange. *Above:* A young girl helps on her family's farm.

won't have to work so hard," she wrote wistfully. But the Great Depression didn't pass quickly. It lasted eleven years.

• • • •

BEFORE THE CRASH

Many youngsters of the Great Depression were born in the 1920s. Times were good then. Herbert Hoover, a self-made millionaire, was president. Men worked, women kept house, and children went to school.

Many Americans of the 1920s ignored the "proper" manners of earlier days. For the first time, women and older girls wore short skirts above the knee. Young people welcomed fast dances like the Charleston, snapped their fingers to a new kind of music called jazz, and saw the first talking movies.

Carefree Americans bought expensive things like houses, cars, and washing machines. To pay for these things, they often borrowed money. By the time the stock market crashed, millions of Americans were in debt.

The crash had a snowball effect. When a business lost money, it had to lay off workers. The unemployed workers stopped paying their debts. They also stopped buying new things. Stores had fewer customers, so factories made fewer products and earned less money. More workers lost their jobs.

Almost overnight, comfortable middle-class families began to struggle financially. The poorest Americans—who only scraped by during good times—became desperately poor. Churches and relief organizations like the Red Cross tried to help. Some opened food centers to feed people who couldn't afford food. Others tried to help people find jobs. But these groups couldn't do enough. Too many people needed help.

....

RICH FAMILIES

Although the Great Depression hurt millions of Americans, some suffered little hardship. People continued to work as lawyers, doctors, and secretaries. They drove buses, ran restaurants, and delivered mail. They could still afford to buy new cars, to travel, and even to throw fancy parties. Some kids still attended expensive private schools and summer camps.

Sometimes the rich looked down on the poor. Many believed that

As their nice clothes show, these children did not go without during the depression.

unemployed people were lazy. But other wealthy families tried to help the needy. One group of New Jersey girls formed the "Secret Helpers Club" and prepared food baskets for poor families. "When we had a box filled with food, we'd put it on the porch, ring the doorbell, and then dash out to the car so our identities would remain a secret," remembered secret helper Toni Johnson.

....

WHEN YOU'RE DOWN AND OUT

Two brothers in Tennessee kept their family from freezing one winter in the early 1930s by stealing firewood from a rich family. Thirteen-year-old Jeems and his older brother sometimes got up in the middle of the night, bundled up against the cold, and trekked with a sled to the rich family's nearby woods. The boys could bring home nine or ten loads of firewood in one night. "Mama never did ask us where the wood came from," Jeems remembered. "She always knew somehow when we were going to do it, and those nights she went to bed early."

Many Americans left their homes in the country, hoping to find work and a better life in the city. But even there, few jobs were available. Desperate and hungry families stole food to survive. Men robbed grocery stores. Children snatched fruit and vegetables from peddlers' carts.

Some Americans could no longer afford to pay for their apartments or houses and became homeless. Before long, homeless families built flimsy shacks for shelter, using wooden crates, tar paper, and other odds and ends. Sometimes groups of families set up their shacks together on the outskirts of a city. These shantytowns were nicknamed Hoovervilles since people blamed President Hoover for the nation's desperate situation.

About two hundred jobless men lived in this Hooverville in New York City, in 1932.

A VISIT TO A HOOVERVILLE

Inez Williamson of Indianapolis, Indiana, was thirteen when her mother died of cancer. Inez's father traveled a lot, so Inez moved in with her grandmother. Inez's grandmother also took in homeless girls, so the house was always full of people. Inez remembered:

Most of the time there was either eight or nine [young-sters] . . . so she'd have to kinda, you know, partial out the good-ies. . . . And we got to grumbling or griping about 'Well, I didn't get this or I didn't get that'. . . . They couldn't always buy a lot of gasoline, so we didn't always get to go in the car very much. Grandma . . . would get as many as we could in the car. And at that time there was a Hooverville on the White River, and they'd take us down there. And those people . . . had all built shacks [on rafts] on the water, and they tied them to the shore so that way they didn't have to pay any taxes. . . . And so when she'd take us down there and say, 'Now, if you kids don't appreciate what you got, just take a look at those children. They don't even have your sweets and your fruits but maybe once a month.' And so it really made us stop and think [about] what we had.

ROOM FOR ONE MORE

Clancy Strock of Illinois remembered that a stream of aunts, uncles, and cousins lived with his family during the depression. Many people like the Strocks opened their homes to relatives who had lost theirs. If there weren't enough beds, "guests" slept on the floor or in the barn. In nice weather, people pitched a tent in the backyard and lived there.

A homeless family in 1936

A house bulging with relatives sometimes led to arguments and less room for everyone. But the extra people provided extra help with child care and household chores. Aunts, uncles, and grandparents entertained younger generations with stories, games, and family traditions.

••••

"FEND FOR YOURSELF"

Sometimes families split up. Clarence Lee was sixteen when his father asked him to leave home. "Go fend for yourself," Mr. Lee told Clarence. "I cannot afford to have you around any longer." As the depression wore on, one quarter of a million American children became homeless tramps. They hitchhiked along the nation's highways and railways, searching for food and shelter.

Young tramps often traveled and lived together for safety. The hobo camps they set up along rivers and near small towns were

HOPPING A FREIGHT CAR

This young man became a hobo at age eighteen. He traveled constantly. But he rarely hitchhiked along highways. "Freights is a lot better," he said. About 200,000 young people were hobos during the depression.

nicknamed "jungles." As in other communities, people in the jungle knew that giving a helping hand almost always meant getting one in return. Young tramps relied on each other instead of on parents and other adults. They knew teamwork would help them survive. Everyone contributed. Some scrounged for firewood, and others found food, water, and other necessary items.

Times were especially hard for homeless kids. But youngsters everywhere felt the sting of the depression. Young folks had to grow up quickly. As the 1930s began, the hardest days of their lives lay ahead.

"Go fend for yourself, I cannot afford to have you around any longer."
—*Mr. Lee to his son, Clarence*

CHAPTER TWO

HOW WELL
CAN WE
LIVE?

"I see one-third of a nation ill-housed,

During the Great Depression, many families struggled to keep jobs and to stay together. They learned to live on less. They made things last longer and go farther, never wasting a crust of bread or a bit of string.

People often traded instead of using money (which they didn't have). Farmers could swap eggs, cream, and butter at the store for coffee, sugar, and flour. Families everywhere traded labor. Instead of paying a worker for a big job like painting a house, neighbors took turns painting each other's homes.

• • • •

"RAGGEDY RAGGEDY ARE WE"

Without money for new clothes, inventive Americans found new uses for what they had on hand. They used string for shoelaces and rope for belts. They slipped cardboard into their shoes when the soles had worn through. Clothes were handed down, patched, and handed down again.

Women sewed clothes from whatever spare fabric they could find. The Salvation Army provided free, used clothing to needy people like the Tathems.

Opposite: A young girl prepares a family meal. *Above:* A resourceful mother wears a flour sack for a skirt.

ill-clad, ill-nourished."

— *President Franklin D. Roosevelt, January 20, 1937*

A talented seamstress, Mrs. Ruby Tathem altered used adult clothing to fit her children.

Farmers bought animal feed in large cotton sacks, and women and girls used the sacks to make shirts, shorts, dish towels, and even underwear. Many sacks came in pretty floral or striped patterns. Often people would buy matching sacks, bringing home enough of one pattern to make a whole dress. Children who didn't have feed sacks or hand-me-downs wore their clothes into threadbare rags that fell to pieces when washed.

• • • •

BEANS, BACON, AND GRAVY

Folks quickly found creative ways to stock the dinner table.

Clancy Strock's parents shopped on Saturday evenings. The grocery

A woman prepares jars of preserved homegrown goods. Living on less money caused many families to find creative ways to stock the shelves.

store wasn't open on Sundays, and some of the food would spoil before Monday. So the grocer cut prices to sell the food on Saturday night.

Some youngsters got jobs to help out. "I give all I earn for food for the family," one girl wrote in a letter. Other children scoured woods and fields for berries, roots, and nuts. They hunted and fished in forests and streams. Each summer Clancy Strock rode his bike along country roads near his home and gathered wild asparagus.

Many families started growing fruits and vegetables in backyard gardens. Youngsters helped their mothers tend the gardens, pick the crops, and can the harvest to preserve the foods for winter.

Some people were less fortunate than the Strocks. During the 1930s, almost 25 percent of the nation's children did not get enough healthy food to eat. They were malnourished. In the poverty-stricken communities of the Appalachian Mountains, 90 percent of the children were malnourished. Some malnourished children kept their stomachs from feeling hollow by eating the red clay earth. "Clay-eaters may be identified by the color and texture of their skin," wrote one journalist in the 1930s, "which looks and feels like putty."

A youngster in Siloam, Georgia, digs for the kind of clay that some people ate.

HUNGRY EVERY DAY

Among the poorest Americans were southern sharecroppers, who
farmed land they did not own. To pay rent on the land, they "shared"
profits from the crops with the landowners. Not much money was
left for the sharecroppers. Even before the depression, entire
sharecropping families worked in the fields to pay the landlord.

Landowners wanted every acre planted with crops such as cotton
that could be sold for cash. Sometimes they would not allow
sharecroppers to raise animals or to grow vegetables to feed their
families. With little money for vegetables, meat, and milk,
sharecropping families often ate only cornmeal and molasses.

Sometimes sharecroppers got a deadly disease called pellagra that
leaves a strange red rash on the body. Scientists knew that poor
diet causes pellagra. But many
who had the disease did not
know how they had gotten
sick or how to get better.
Nicknamed the "red shame,"
pellagra killed seven thousand
Americans each year between
1927 and 1937.

Red Cross workers often
talked to landowners,
explaining the importance of
letting families have a small
plot of land to grow vegetables
for their family. These gardens
became known as "lifesaving
gardens."

This toddler's legs are curved—
a sign of malnutrition.

A GOOD ROAD TO FOLLOW

Homeless youth traveled from one place to another, seeking enough food for one more day and a place to sleep for one more night. Once in a while, they even found a bath and a change of clothes.

Slowly, hobos developed their own written language—a loose system of symbols *(below)*. They left messages for each other by drawing these symbols on sidewalks, fences, and walls. A message might tell other hobos if a specific farm or business was a good place to ask for food and work. Other messages warned hobos to stay away from places that didn't welcome strangers.

Lucille Boyatt remembered the many hobos who came to her Idaho home looking for food and work during the 1930s. Lucille's mother believed their home had been marked as a friendly place. She was probably right.

....

PRESIDENT ROOSEVELT'S ALPHABET SOUP

Franklin Delano Roosevelt (FDR) became president in 1933. He promised a New Deal—or a better life—for Americans. He created jobs and programs to help them. FDR's New Deal programs were nicknamed "alphabet soup" because their long formal names often got shortened to initials. For example, the National Youth Administration, which helped youngsters in many ways, was called the NYA.

In the early months of President Roosevelt's New Deal, the government offered needy people free food, free clothes, or sometimes even cash. New Deal programs helped put banks back in business and helped keep kids in school.

President Roosevelt and one of his many grandchildren

THE MARCH OF DIMES

In the 1930s, polio was a serious disease that crippled thousands of children. Some children died. President Franklin Roosevelt got polio as an adult. He survived. But he could walk only with leg braces after that.

In 1935 about 17,000 children took a newly developed vaccine against polio. Some of them got polio anyway. To help find a better vaccine, Americans sent almost three million dimes to the National Foundation for Infantile Paralysis in 1938. The March of Dimes became an ongoing effort that eventually helped scientists develop an improved vaccine.

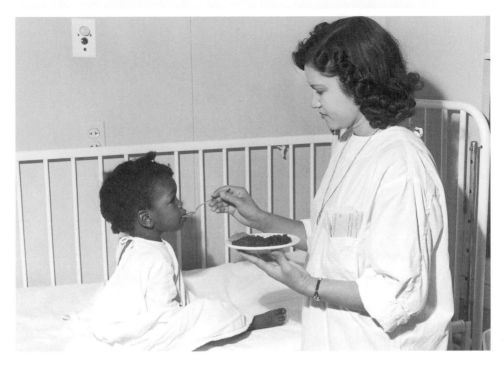

A sick little girl in a hospital in Eleven Mile Corner, Arizona, eats with help from a young woman from the National Youth Administration.

And they helped get people back to work. Several New Deal programs hired men to build public roads, bridges, and dams. Former businessmen who had no money to buy work clothes swung a shovel in a suit and tie. New Deal programs also hired women to work as librarians, secretaries, seamstresses, and school-lunch cooks. Even artists found jobs. The government hired them to produce artwork such as posters with a public service message.

The government created jobs for some artists by hiring them to make posters like this one.

CHAPTER THREE

OLD DUST STORM GOT MY FAMILY

"You better git out quick or it will smother you."

—*"Why We Come to Californy," a song by Flora Robertson Shafter, 1940*

• •

Beginning in the early 1930s, drought (dry weather) settled over the southwestern United States. The hardest hit areas were Oklahoma and parts of Texas and Kansas. The drought killed crops, year after year.

The bare soil was so dry that it blew away easily in the wind. By the mid-1930s, southwestern towns and farms were blanketed with layers of suffocating dust. In one storm, 350 million tons of soil blew from the southwest to the east. The huge region of dry, dusty land became known as the Dust Bowl.

Some children living in these clouds of dust suffered from "dust pneumonia." They got so much dust in their lungs that they found it hard to breathe, even indoors.

Folksinger Woody Guthrie wrote songs about Americans who battled the dust. In "Dust Can't Kill Me," Guthrie sang, "The old dust storm killed my baby/Can't kill me, Lord/Can't kill me./That old dust storm got my family/Can't get me, Lord/Can't get me."

Opposite: This famous photograph of an Oklahoma dust storm in 1936 was taken by Arthur Rothstein. *Above:* An Oklahoma boy covers his face to keep out the dusty air.

Families who were forced to move away from the Dust Bowl took as many of their belongings as they could.

. . . .

"OKIES"

Almost one million Americans fled the Dust Bowl and headed west to California and Oregon. They followed rumors that fruit and vegetable growers in the West would hire almost anyone. With barely enough money for gasoline, families stashed their belongings onto pickup trucks. They packed in too many passengers and crossed their fingers as they drove west. So many people fleeing the Dust Bowl came from Oklahoma that Dust Bowl refugees became known as Okies.

Oca and Ruby Tathem and their children left their Oklahoma home for California in 1933. At the Oklahoma border, their rickety pickup truck passed a sign that California government workers had put up. The sign read: "No jobs in California. If you are out of work, keep out."

"If you are out of work, keep out."

—a sign posted by the state of California, 1933

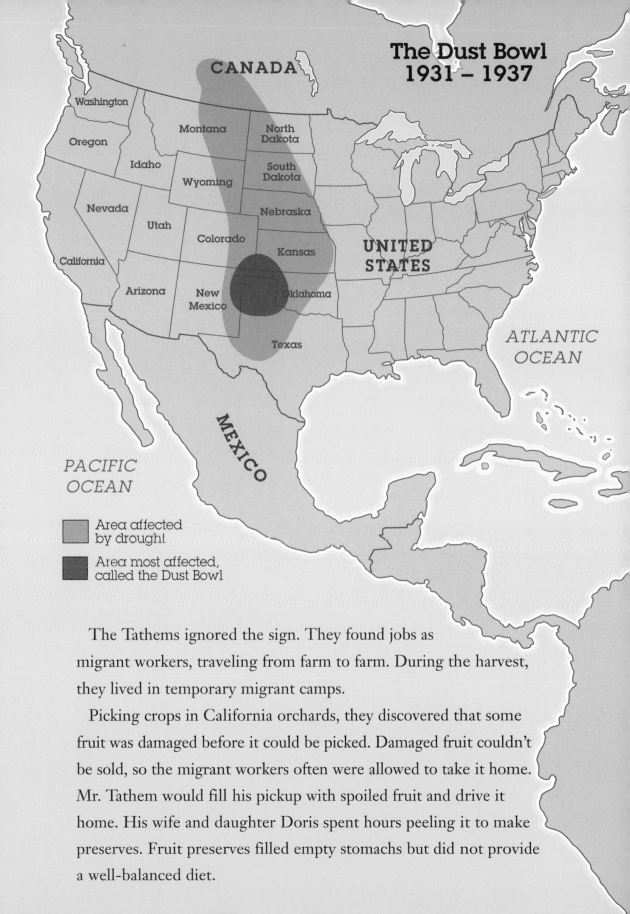

CANADA

Washington

Oregon

Montana

North
Dakota

Idaho

South
Dakota

Wyoming

Nevada

Nebraska

Utah

Colorado

California

Kansas

UNITED
STATES

Arizona

New
Mexico

Oklahoma

Texas

ATLANTIC
OCEAN

MEXICO

PACIFIC
OCEAN

Area affected
by drought

Area most affected,
called the Dust Bowl

The Tathems ignored the sign. They found jobs as migrant workers, traveling from farm to farm. During the harvest, they lived in temporary migrant camps.

Picking crops in California orchards, they discovered that some fruit was damaged before it could be picked. Damaged fruit couldn't be sold, so the migrant workers often were allowed to take it home. Mr. Tathem would fill his pickup with spoiled fruit and drive it home. His wife and daughter Doris spent hours peeling it to make preserves. Fruit preserves filled empty stomachs but did not provide a well-balanced diet.

WHY WE COME TO CALIFORNY

song by Flora Robertson Shafter, 1940

Here comes the dust-storm
Watch the sky turn blue.
You better git out quick
Or it will smother you.

Californy, Californy,
Here I come too.
With a coffee pot and skillet,
I'm a-comin' to you!

Migrant workers moved often, looking for work in orchards and fields.
They often had a tent for a home.

Like Joe Montgomery, these children lived in a camp for migrant workers built by the U.S. government.

• • • •

A ROOF OVER OUR HEADS

Under President Roosevelt's New Deal, the U.S. government began building camps where migrant workers could live. The people living in a camp paid about one dollar per week to stay there. Everyone shared jobs such as cleaning the restrooms. Youngsters organized ball teams. People got together on Saturday nights for dances.

In the mid-1930s, Joe Montgomery traveled with his parents and sisters and brothers to the Arvin Federal Government Camp in California. The houses were simple cabins and tents. But at least the camp offered hot showers, flush toilets, and plenty of food that the Montgomerys "greatly appreciated." They spent a year in all at the camp.

CHAPTER FOUR

ALL
WRONG
FOR
WRITING

"I am in the seventh grade in school but have to stay out of school because I have [no] books or clothes to ware."

— a thirteen-year-old Arkansas girl in a letter to First Lady Eleanor Roosevelt, 1936

● ●

During the Great Depression, almost half of American youths were neither in school nor working. There were many reasons to leave school. For example, many schools cut down on hours or closed because they didn't have enough money to stay open. In 1933 Alabama closed most of its schools.

Some children couldn't get to school. They lived too far away to walk. And their parents couldn't take them, since the family car, wagon, horse, or bicycles had been sold for cash.

Other youngsters left school because they could not afford to buy coats and boots for winter and shoes for the rest of the year. Others were ashamed of their tattered, patched, and mismatched clothes. Loraine Johnson of Idaho remembered that her father couldn't afford to buy her boots during the Great Depression. All through the winter, her father wrapped heavy burlap over her shoes, then walked her to the bus stop. Before the bus arrived, he removed the

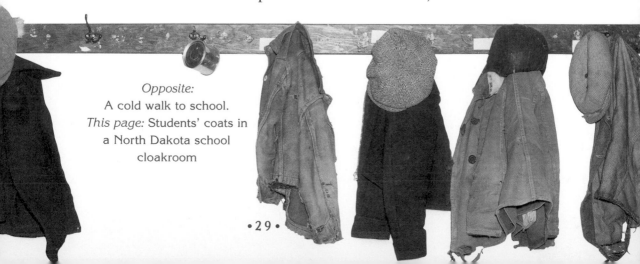

Opposite:
A cold walk to school.
This page: Students' coats in
a North Dakota school
cloakroom

•29•

ugly burlap bags. "He didn't want us to be embarrassed," Loraine remembered. "Neither did he want us to freeze our feet."

• • • •

"DEAR MRS. ROOSEVELT"

Thousands of American youth looked to First Lady Eleanor Roosevelt for help. She understood their problems and was determined to help them. On the radio and in a newspaper column called "My Day," she explained how the depression affected American youth.

At a Christmas party, First Lady Eleanor Roosevelt visited with boys from unemployed families.

Throughout the depression, young people wrote to Mrs. Roosevelt asking for help. Some asked for bikes so they could get to school and work. Some begged for hand-me-downs to replace worn-out clothing. Some needed money to pay medical bills and to buy food and school supplies.

One girl wrote in 1935, "I graduate this year and I haven't enough money to buy a dress. . . . I hate to go on the stage with the other girls in my shabby dress." The following year, a girl in Arkansas wrote, "I am writing you for some of your old soiled dress[es] if you have any. I am a poor girl who has to stay out of schol on account of dresses, and slips, and a coat."

Many youngsters were disappointed when they learned that Mrs. Roosevelt could not send bikes, clothes, and money to everyone who asked. They had to be content knowing she was doing the best she could.

NO TIME FOR SCHOOL

Many families needed their children's help much of the year to earn money. Going to school was not as important. For example, the children of southern sharecroppers worked in the fields. If the family didn't plant and pick enough crops, they wouldn't earn enough to pay the rent. Then the landlord would kick them out of their homes. The children of migrant workers also had to work in the fields.

Tom and his older brother Pete were sharecropper's sons from Alabama. For most of the year, they had to work in the fields. In winter, they went to a school for African Americans only. But they had to take turns going to school because they had only one pair of shoes between them.

When sharecropping and migrant children did attend schools, they struggled to keep up. Since their attendance was poor, their skills

Plowing was a family affair for these farm children in Heard County, Georgia.

were not as far along as the other students' skills. Some teachers treated migrant students badly. Schoolmates made fun of their shabby clothes and poor lunches. Discouraged, many migrant children dropped out of school and spent their time waiting for the harvest.

Before moving to California, Cleo and Ophelia Tathem struggled to go to school in their Oklahoma town. The school couldn't afford supplies for the students, so parents had to buy them. But the Tathems had little money for school supplies. Ophelia tried hard to make her last tablet of Big Chief writing paper last as long as she could. She made her handwriting as small as possible and used the back of every page for her homework. But eventually she filled the tablet. With no money for more school supplies, both Cleo and Ophelia were forced to quit school.

After the Tathems moved to California, the younger children attended school while the older ones picked crops alongside the adults. Ophelia wore hand-me-down clothes to school. She

Just like modern youngsters, these Maryland students are studying division.

WEEDPATCH CAMP

The Arvin Federal Government Camp for migrant workers was located in Kern County, California. The children who lived at the Weedpatch Camp, as it was often called, attended public schools in the county. But some parents and teachers didn't want the Weedpatch children there. Superintendent of schools Leo Hart believed the camp children deserved a decent education. So Hart, fifty Weedpatch children, and eight teachers built their own school in 1940. Using scrap lumber and other free materials, they did their own carpentry, plumbing, and wiring. They even raised vegetables and cows for the school's food and milk.

remembered feeling shabby around the California girls who lived in town. Ophelia couldn't go to birthday parties or skating parties because she couldn't afford to buy gifts or rent skates.

....

HARD TIMES FOR TEACHERS

In many places, teachers' salaries were lowered. Some teachers were paid in "scrip," a money substitute. Teachers could use scrip to pay for items at stores. Merchants accepted scrip, but only grudgingly. Eventually many teachers across the country were not paid at all.

> *"Miss Lundeen is left with 15 c[ents] and is in debt for clothes she charged. . . ."*
>
> —*Ann Marie Low, writing about her teacher*

Some unpaid Alabama teachers lost their homes and had to live in school buildings. In North Dakota, one of Ann Marie Low's teachers lost her life savings when the local bank closed. "Miss Lundeen is left with 15 c[ents] and is in debt for clothes she

In this one-room school, students cook their own lunch.

charged in Minneapolis," Ann Marie wrote in her diary.

Some teachers went on strike (refused to go to work each day), protesting low wages and poor teaching materials. Others took what teaching jobs they could find, no matter how harsh the conditions or how low the pay. They were grateful to have a job at all.

In 1932 and 1933, Bob Simonson's mother, Dorothy Simonson, accepted a teaching job on Isle Royale, a remote island in Lake Superior. Bob and his mother lived in the log cabin school without electricity or running water. In the winter, outdoor temperatures dipped far below zero. Bob and his mother had to huddle around the wood stove to stay warm.

Dorothy Simonson had few teaching supplies. "I realize now how little material we really have," she complained in her journal. "The blackboard is so small and so awkward to use: the tables and chairs are all wrong for writing. . . . Our makeshift devices are pathetically amusing: bottle tops for arithmetic counters, flash cards out of advertising cards, and stencils from candy boxes!"

> *"The blackboard is so small and so awkward to use: the tables and chairs are all wrong for writing."*
> —*Dorothy Simonson, 1933*

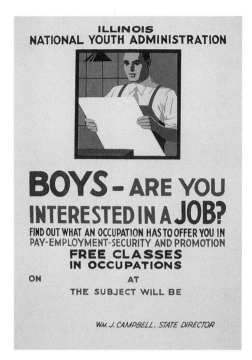

The National Youth Administration helped both boys and girls in many ways. These posters advertise classes that teach job skills.

• • • •

HELP FOR YOUTH

In the 1932 to 1933 school year, many college students found they could not pay tuition and other college costs. More than eighty thousand students dropped out of college that year. President Roosevelt's National Youth Administration (NYA) helped them. It loaned money for college expenses to almost half a million students. The NYA also gave part-time jobs to more than two million high school and college students. With this help, students could go to school and still earn money for their families.

CHAPTER FIVE

HARD WORK
IN
HARD TIMES

Been a workin' in the Army,
Workin' on a farm,
All I got to show for it
Is the muscle in my arm.

—"Wanderin'," an American folk song

By the mid-1930s, President Roosevelt's programs were beginning to help people. But fourteen to fifteen million Americans were still without jobs. Another forty million did not work regularly. Unemployment lines stretched down the nation's streets, while unemployed workers waited patiently outside any business that might be hiring.

• • • •

CHANGING FAMILY ROLES

In the 1930s, men were the main "breadwinners" in American families. When husbands and fathers lost their jobs, they hated to see their wives and children go to work.

But when a family needed money, women and children did what they could to earn it. Women cleaned houses and took in laundry and sewing. Youngsters sold homegrown fruits and vegetables. They set up stands by the side of the road, or they carted the produce door to door in wagons. Girls became baby-sitters. They also worked as "hired girls," helping well-to-do families with household chores. Boys trapped animals and sold the fur for money. When Clancy Strock was eleven, he worked alongside his father shoveling snow on county roads for one dollar a day.

To earn extra money, Ann Marie Low typed letters for the school superintendent in her town. She bought her own typewriter shortly before the local bank closed and all customers lost their

Opposite: A discouraged young man, 1930s. *Above:* Ann Marie Low bought a typewriter like this one.

WPA DOLLS

The Works Progress Administration (WPA) started many projects so that Americans would have jobs. One project was in Milwaukee, Wisconsin. The Milwaukee Handicraft Project hired hundreds of workers (mostly women). The women created many handmade toys such as cloth dolls. The dolls were sold to children's hospitals, orphanages, and other institutions for children. The project made no profit. It sold the dolls for the cost of materials only. First Lady Eleanor Roosevelt visited the project on November 12, 1936. In her newspaper column, "My Day," she wrote, "They are making dolls as attractive as any I have seen."

Mrs. Roosevelt admired the dolls made by the Milwaukee Handicraft Project.

savings. "It is lucky I bought the typewriter," she wrote in her journal. "The rest of my money is gone. Typewriters are as scarce in this town as people who can type." With her earnings she bought clothes, school supplies, and other things her parents could no longer afford.

A teenage worker in the South supported his family for a while by pumping gas and painting houses. But the paint fumes made him sick. So he found factory work making shoes and overalls. "My money has to go a long way," he told a writer in the mid-1930s. "I've got to pay eight dollars a month rent and I have to buy coal for the woodstove. I got to buy clothes for the family and something to eat. All of my family has weak eyes, but we can't afford to wear glasses."

"I got to buy clothes for the family and something to eat."
—*working teenager, mid-1930s*

"Newsies" worked hard to sell their newspapers.
Some helped support their families this way.

NEWSIES

Some boys and young men found work as newsboys. Parked on almost every city corner, these workers sold newspapers. Before selling the papers, "newsies" had to buy them from the publisher. If a newsie and his family could scrape together enough money for a good supply of papers, the newsie stood to make a nice profit.

With a pile of papers at his feet, a newsboy would cry, "Extra! Extra! Read all about it," hoping a passerby would stop and buy a paper. Nine-year-old Don Blincoe sold papers in Jacksonville, Florida. His best customers were Sears shoppers and employees who came out of the Sears store on his corner. "We gave our earnings to mom every night," he remembered.

Many young factory workers were paid by the number of "pieces" they made. A worker who assembled fifty shoes an hour might earn eleven dollars a week. If he worked more slowly, he earned less. "Piecework" later became illegal because it did not provide workers with a steady amount of money.

Many city families earned a living by working for factories, but they did the work at home. Mothers, fathers, and youngsters sewed buttons onto cards, slid bobby pins into packages, or bunched safety pins. "We all sit around the table and work as fast as we can," a young girl told a child advocate (an adult checking up on the treatment of children) in the early 1930s. "It is very tiring to the eyes and nerves." Working six hours a night for a week, a family of six or more people might make four dollars. Children who worked at home or in factory sweatshops earned only pennies an hour.

• • • •

IN THE FIELDS

In sharecropping families, everyone had to work so that the family could survive. Children as young as six picked cotton.

Children in sharecropping families grew up fast working alongside adults.

A sharecropper's son named Tom picked cotton alongside his older brother and their parents. The boys worked twelve hours a day in one-hundred-degree weather. Their five-year-old sister, Jenny, cleaned house and looked after younger siblings.

About two million men, women, and children worked as migrant farmworkers during the depression. Before the Tathems of Oklahoma moved to California, they picked cotton as migrant workers. Three-year-old Doris and one-year-old Dick accompanied their parents and their seventeen-year-old Aunt Cleo to the fields. While the adults worked, the children often slept on an old flour sack under the shade of a tree. Sometimes Mrs. Tathem pulled the little ones in a cart along the rows as she picked.

This sixteen-year-old earned two dollars a day as a pea picker.

Homeless youngsters found odd jobs when they could. They often worked for a day or two on farms or in other places in exchange for a hot meal, a soapy bath, and a place to spend the night. One young hobo from Pennsylvania known only as Blink worked his way across the country. He recorded his odd jobs in his journal. Once he helped a truck driver unload his truck. He also washed walls at a soup kitchen, cleaned a basement, cut grass, and did farm chores. He learned some useful lessons from a new friend in August 1932. "Met Al," Blink wrote in his journal. "Showed me how to get seven free meals a day."

CHAPTER SIX

DREAMS
FOR A
DIME

"Please don't forget us. We will be waiting for you Christmas Day."

—a New York boy, in a letter sent to Santa Claus, 1932

For many children, birthdays and holidays in the 1930s weren't much different from ordinary days. Farmwork had to be done every day of the year, so Ann Marie and Bud Low spent holidays working alongside their father. At that time, Will Rogers was a popular humorist who made everybody laugh. "Some people are having a little trouble scraping up a reason for Thanksgiving this year," he quipped in 1930. "Some think we ought to skip a year and put on a big one in 1931."

But some families did manage to celebrate Thanksgiving and other holidays. They hoarded expensive items like sugar to make a cake or other treat. And trick-or-treaters could still have fun on Halloween. They dumped garbage on front porches or rang doorbells, running away before anyone answered. Other kids ran screaming through neighborhoods. Articles in women's magazines showed how to make inexpensive Halloween costumes from scraps of fabric.

••••

TIGHT CHRISTMAS

For Hanukkah and Christmas, parents whittled toys and figurines from wood scraps and sewed doll clothes from rags as gifts. A grandmother might unravel an old sweater to knit scarves and mittens. Many adults who grew up during the depression later remembered that these homemade gifts meant more than any store-bought gift they ever received.

Opposite: Some families did not have to skimp at Christmas in the 1930s. *Above:* A store-bought toy train

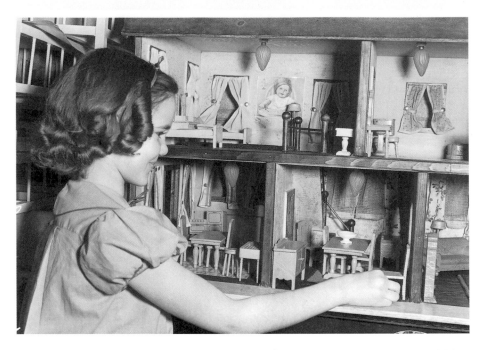

A handmade dollhouse and dolls meant magical fun for many girls in the 1930s.

Clancy Strock of Illinois remembered a December when his father spent a suspicious amount of time in the family's basement. When Christmas Day finally arrived, Clancy and his sister discovered why. "He had constructed a miniature kitchen cupboard from an orange crate for my sister," Clancy remembered. "My gift was a checkerboard made from a piece of plywood accompanied by a set of wooden chessmen."

The Strocks always had a Christmas tree, thanks to Mr. Strock's quick thinking. He would wait until the last Christmas tree seller was about to close his stand on Christmas Eve. Then Mr. Strock made his move. "The trees that were left were scraggly, ugly lopsided ones with missing branches and bent trunks," Clancy remembered. "The seller was happy to settle for 25 cents and close up shop." The Strock family then enjoyed decorating the sorry tree until it was beautiful.

One poor sharecropping family, the Turners of South Carolina, didn't have Christmas at all during the Great Depression. Like other sharecroppers, they were grateful to go to bed with stomachs that didn't rumble with hunger. "We h'aint had no Christmas here," Mrs. Turner said. "Not an apple, a nut, or nothing." One year she asked the landlord for extra money to buy some clothes and a few cheap gifts for the children. "Mr. Anderson said we shouldn't have the money," Mrs. Turner remembered, "and told us to move."

> "We h'aint had no Christmas here. Not an apple, a nut, or nothing."
>
> —Mrs. Turner, a mother in a sharecropping family, 1930s

• • • •

"DEAR SANTA CLAUS"

Throughout the Great Depression, children wrote to Santa Claus. Many asked Santa for jobs, money, or schoolbooks instead of toys and games. Some children mailed their letters to the White House in Washington, D.C. They hoped that President Roosevelt, who cared so much about Americans, could somehow get their Christmas wishes to Santa Claus.

In 1932 about five thousand Santa Claus letters ended up in the New York City central post office. The *New York Times* newspaper published some of the letters. Many were written on dirty scraps of paper. Some arrived in homemade envelopes without stamps.

> "To Santa Clause in the Happy Land where there is no Depression."
>
> —address on a letter to Santa

One was addressed to "Santa Clause in the Happy Land where there is no Depression." A New York City boy, whose family often went to bed hungry, pleaded, "Please don't forget us. We will be waiting for you

Christmas Day." The post office asked for help to answer some of the letters. Five hundred families volunteered. They wrote notes or sent gifts to the letter writers, helping to make their Christmas wishes come true.

• • • •

PASTIMES

Despite their troubles, American families found ways to have fun. Children made up games using sticks, rocks, and other things they found. Old magazines were handy. Girls cut paper dolls from magazine pictures of models. They pasted them on scraps of cardboard and dressed them in magazine clothes. Games that required no materials—such as pom-pom pullaway, hide-and-seek, and tag—were also popular.

In 1936, when Doris Tathem of California was six, her parents gave her an allowance of one nickel each week. Every week she

A group of children played leapfrog in Harlem, a neighborhood in New York City, 1930.

Kids gathered in the neighborhood sandlot for a game of stickball.

thought for a long time before she spent it. Sometimes she bought an ice cream cone or a pencil and a pack of gum. Other times she saved her nickles for a movie, which cost ten or fifteen cents.

• • • •

"WHERE LIFE IS BETTER"

Televisions were not invented until after the depression. But radios provided hours of free entertainment. During the day, adults listened to soap opera dramas on the radio. In the afternoon, children tuned in to adventure shows such as *The Green Hornet* and *The Lone Ranger*. After dinner, the entire family gathered around the radio for popular series such as *Our Gal Sunday*. Listeners tapped their toes to the sounds of swing music. They chuckled along with variety shows, similar to modern television talk shows.

Youngsters and adults both enjoyed the newspaper comics. Somehow, reading about the adventures of Dick Tracy and Little Orphan Annie made Americans feel better. There was no depression in the funny pages.

A teenage factory worker in the South enjoyed relaxing with the comics after work. "The Tarzan part. That's the best thing in the funny papers," he told a writer in 1936. "Nobody ever gets it over old Tarzan, do they?"

"Nobody ever gets it over old Tarzan, do they?"

—*teenage factory worker*

BATMAN IS BORN

The nation's first comic book was produced in 1933. It was a softcover magazine with thirty-two pages full of comic strips that had appeared in newspapers. The first comic book series to use original comic strips appeared in 1936. Called Detective Picture Stories, it focused on one theme—solving crime—the way modern comic books focus on a theme. By 1938 superheroes were dominating comic books. They included Superman, Captain Marvel, and Batman.

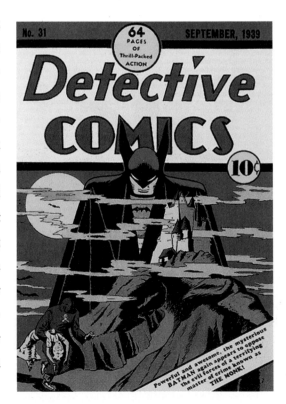

HOPALONG CASSIDY'S CREED

American youngsters of the 1930s loved movie westerns. One popular movie cowboy was named Hopalong Cassidy. In fifty-four movies made between 1935 and 1943, Hopalong battled crime with his quick shooting and strong character. He gave American youngsters the following rules to live by.

The highest badge of honor a person can wear is honesty. Be truthful at all times.

Your parents are the best friends you have. Listen to them and obey their instructions.

If you want to be respected, you must respect others. Show good manners in every way.

Only through hard work and study can you succeed. Don't be lazy.

Your good deeds always come to light. So don't boast or be a show-off.

If you waste time or money today, you will regret it tomorrow. Practice thrift in all ways.

A strong, healthy body is a precious gift. Be neat and clean.

Our country's laws are made for your protection. Observe them carefully.

Children in many foreign lands are less fortunate than you. Be glad and proud you are an American.

Escaping to the movies was another popular pastime. During the depression, almost 60 percent of Americans attended the movies every week. Movie theaters showed double features and organized contests with prizes ranging from cash to food baskets.

Depression-era movies did not reflect the hard times of everyday life. Instead, they often showed happy days. Happy endings made everyone feel better. Motion picture companies made musicals, comedies, and dramas based on familiar stories such as *Little Women* and *The Wizard of Oz*.

Even Blink, the young hobo from Pennsylvania, could sometimes collect enough change for a good time. "Made 80c helping guy build fence," he wrote in his journal in 1932. "Spent 5c for ice cream cone. 10c for movie. Swell show. All about gangsters and true to life."

"Spent 5c for ice cream cone. 10c for movie. Swell show."

—*Blink, a young hobo, 1932*

Even during the hard times of the depression, American youngsters flocked to the movies.

SHIRLEY TEMPLE

Shirley Temple was a child movie star who charmed moviegoers with her corkscrew curls, dimples, and song-and-dance routines. For many Americans, she was a ray of hope. Her personality was as cheery as her smile. Americans loved her. Between 1931 and 1939, Shirley made more than forty movies, including *Heidi* and *The Little Princess.* President Roosevelt

Child star Shirley Temple, 1934. Shirley started acting at age three.

praised Shirley Temple by saying, "When the spirit of the American people is lower than at any other time during the Depression, it is a splendid thing that for just 15 cents, an American can go to a movie and look at the smiling face of [Shirley Temple] and forget his troubles."

PHENOMENAL EARNINGS

In the depression, waitresses made about $520 a year. Coal miners brought home a little more than $700. Doctors earned about $3,500. Shirley Temple's salary was $300,000 a year during the 1930s. Still more money came from the sale of Shirley Temple dolls, toys, and hair products.

CHAPTER SEVEN

GROWN
AND
GONE

"I'm going down,
I'm going down to the CCC."

—"CCC Blues," a depression-era song about the Civilian Conservation
Corps, by Washboard Sam

Worn down by the depression's many hardships, some American youth entered adulthood discouraged. Some bright students received scholarships to colleges. Others found jobs and paid their own way.

The Low children—Ann Marie, Bud, and Ethel—worked their way through college. Ann Marie was the first to graduate. She found a job as a teacher and helped pay the bills for Bud and Ethel. Sometimes their father had to borrow money to help pay for their college costs. In April 1931, times were particularly tight for Ann Marie and Ethel. "We had hoped to get a cream check [money from selling cream] yesterday, but didn't," Ann Marie wrote in her journal. "We are destitute."

Many young people wanted to marry but didn't because they could not afford to set up their own household or support a family. Unable to lead independent lives, many young people were uncertain about their futures. In many cases, families relied on the income of adult children living at home.

• • • •

HAPPY DAYS IN THE CCC

One of President Roosevelt's programs helped unemployed young men. Run by the U.S. Army, the Civilian Conservation Corps (CCC) put young men (aged seventeen to twenty-eight) to work.

Opposite: Young men bound for adventure in a CCC camp. *Right:* As this poster promised, the CCC offered young men many opportunities.

These men are gathered for "mess" (mealtime) at a CCC camp in New Jersey in 1933.

Almost three million young men lived and worked in more than fifteen hundred CCC camps across the nation. Many of these camps were in national parks and forests. CCC workers planted nearly two hundred million trees. They built fire towers to help prevent forest fires. They dug fishponds, repaired park roads, and restored historic battlefields. CCC workers earned thirty dollars a month. The law required them to send twenty-five dollars home every month. The extra cash helped many American families pay bills and make ends meet.

In the army-style CCC camps, young men made new friends and learned hard work and discipline. And they gained valuable skills. Ann Marie Low's future husband worked for the CCC in North Dakota. The training he received prepared him for a career in wildlife management. CCC workers were also given a chance to learn to read and write. Almost sixty thousand workers did just that. Years later, former CCC workers looked back on their time in camp as happy days.

"JUMP, JIVE, 'N WAIL"

Many young people had little money during the Great Depression. They couldn't afford to think about getting married. But teenagers still dated and fell in love. And some did get married.

Many teenagers listened to a style of jazz music called swing. Teens loved to spend a night out together, dancing to swing. One wildly popular swing dance was the jitterbug. Teens kicked their legs high in this energetic dance.

Probably the best place in the country to dance the jitterbug was the Savoy Ballroom in Harlem, New York. At the Savoy, Saturday nights brought heated dance competitions. Young people made up new steps as they went along, trying to beat the other dancers.

"Jump, Jive 'n Wail" was the name of one swing song. Its lyrics included these words: "You gotta jump, jive, and then you wail/You gotta jump, jive, and then you wail/Mama's in the backyard learning how to jive and wail."

In the late 1990s, the Gap clothing store ran a TV commercial featuring this song. Young actors in the commercial did high-energy dance steps that were very similar to the jitterbug.

The jitterbug is a lively dance that teenagers loved. Some parents thought it was too wild.

GOING TO WAR

Seven years after the depression had begun, Ann Marie Low paused on New Year's Day to consider her future. "Somehow we've made it so far," she wrote in her journal. "Surely in 1936 things will break for the better."

But the depression did not end until about 1941, after the United States entered World War II. Young men were drafted into the U.S. Army, Marines, and Air Corps. The U.S. government hired millions of Americans to make weapons and other war materials in factories. With these boosts, the unemployment rate quickly dropped.

As more and more young men were called into military service,

"Somehow we've made it so far. Surely in 1936 things will break for the better."
—*Ann Marie Low*

Grim news of war in Europe greeted youngsters nearing adulthood in the late 1930s.

young women took over their factory jobs. Some women joined men on the battlefields, working as nurses. The children of the Great Depression were growing up fast.

. . . .

LIFE LESSONS

The memory of hard times never faded for many children of the Great Depression. As adults, they

Even though times were hard during the Great Depression,
young couples still fell in love and got married.

found it hard to waste food, throw things away, or spend money on luxury items.

Children and young people accepted the challenges of the 1930s. Many even felt they had benefited in some ways. Young adults who supported their families, for example, learned to be responsible. When they had their own families, they managed the household income well. They saved their money instead of buying on credit. Youngsters who had survived hard times also learned that they could overcome obstacles and master tough situations. Best of all, they learned that even when life is hard, hope can make a difference.

ACTIVITIES

Study Historical Illustrations

The photographs in this book were made in the 1930s. Many were taken by photographers hired by the Farm Security Administration (FSA). The FSA was a New Deal program that helped farmers and other people. The FSA used photographs to show Congress that FSA programs were needed. As the FSA photographers traveled, they wrote notes about the people they met.

Turn back to page 15. Carl Mydans took this FSA photograph of a young mother and children in Tennessee in March 1936. The family had seven children. The oldest was a seventeen-year-old boy who had only two years of schooling. The father was an unemployed woodcutter. For a home, the family rented a one-room hut made of rough boards. It was located in an open field near a highway. The family cooked their meals on a wood stove in a lean-to shack near their hut. Their only water came from a creek that ran along the highway. Carl Mydans visited them along with a federal worker who had come to help them.

When you study a historical photograph, think about more than just what you see. Also ask questions about what you can't see. Who made the photograph? Why? Was it created to show a certain point of view or to make viewers feel a certain way? How did Carl Mydans want people to feel about the family in Tennessee?

The Library of Congress maintains a website called the Learning Page. One lesson on the Learning Page is called "Brother, Can You Spare a Dime." It includes many FSA photographs and asks questions such as: What is happening in this picture? What are the circumstances this photo represents? How are the people dressed? What can you learn from the expression on their faces? Is there anything interesting or surprising about the situation? What problems or frustrations are suggested by this picture? How are the people adapting to their situation? What help seems to be needed here? What is unique about this image that the photographer wanted to capture? To visit this site, go to <http://lcweb2.loc.gov/learn/lessons/98/dime/student.html>.

Try discussing other photographs in this book with a partner. Make a list of things you see. Working together, write a short paragraph that describes what you can learn from each photograph.

Play Pom-Pom Pullaway

Depression-era children often played games that didn't require expensive equipment. Pom-pom pullaway was a favorite.

To play, find a wide space with plenty of room for running. Gather six or more players. Divide them into two groups. Have the two groups line up on opposite sides of the wide space.

Then choose one person to be It. It stands in the middle between the two groups, then starts the game by calling out: "(Jimmy), pom-pom pullaway. Come away or I'll pull you away."

The player who is called (in this case, Jimmy) starts running across the space. It tries to tag him/her. If the runner gets to the opposite side without being tagged, he/she is safe. But if the runner gets tagged, he/she stays in the middle and helps tag other players. The game continues until only one safe player is left. That player becomes It in the next game.

Declare War

Playing cards was also a cheap form of entertainment. Go Fish, Solitaire, 52 Card Pick Up, and War were all popular games. Here are the rules for War, a game for two players.

First deal all the cards (each player should have twenty-six). Don't look at the cards. Each player places his/her cards in a stack, face down. Both players then turn over the first card in their stack. The player with the highest card takes both cards and adds them to the bottom of his/her stack. Sometimes players turn up matching cards (for example, two aces—the highest possible card). Then they declare war. In a war, each player turns over the card that comes next after the matching card. The player with the highest card takes all four of the played cards. The game continues until one player has all the cards.

Make Magazine Paper Dolls

Store-bought paper dolls were too expensive for many depression-era families. So youngsters made their own paper dolls from old magazines. Here's how. Draw an outline of a person on a piece of cardboard. Then cut around the outline. Color in a face and hair. Look through old magazines for clothes that would fit the paper doll. Cut out the clothes. Be sure to cut tabs to keep the clothes on the doll.

Eat Hobo Food

People had to be creative about meals during the depression. Some ate dandelion greens. In Massachusetts, Anthony Cordone's mother boiled dandelion greens and then put them in sandwiches.

Beans were another cheap food. Beans were especially popular with hobos, since beans could be heated in the can over a campfire. Hobos who didn't own silverware invented bean sandwiches.

BEAN SANDWICHES

Serves two or more

Cut a loaf of unsliced bread in half the short way.

Hollow out part of each half.

Dump a can of beans into a Crock-Pot or into a pan.

Heat the beans in the Crock-Pot or on a stove. Use medium heat.

Fill each hollow bread half with warm beans.

Eat.

Hobos often lived together in temporary camps called jungles. Most jungles kept a pot of stew simmering over an open fire. Any hobo could earn a serving by contributing an ingredient. Usually hobos donated vegetables, fruits, and beans. Every so often, a lucky hobo found a chicken or a rabbit for the pot.

To make hobo stew at home or at school, have each dinner guest bring one ingredient. Choose a vegetable, cooked meat, salt and pepper, or some herbs. Real hobos couldn't plan the exact recipe. Their stews were "potluck."

HOBO STEW

Feeds a jungle

Put the ingredients in a large pot.

Add 1–3 cups of water or enough to cover.

Simmer covered for about one hour on low to medium heat.

Stir occasionally.

Add more water if more servings are needed.

Try Bartering

Without money to pay for things, people in the Great Depression often bartered (traded) for what they needed. Imagine that you and your friends have no money. Then barter with each other for something you need.

Try this idea for bartering in a large group such as a class. Give everyone two or three index cards. On each card, each person should draw and label a service he/she could offer (such as carrying someone's lunchroom tray or helping them with math). Sign your names on the cards.

Then display all the cards on a table. Pick one that shows a service you would like to have. Find the person who is offering the service and barter one of your cards for it. See if everyone can trade at least one service for another.

SOURCE NOTES

  6 Ann Marie Low, *Dustbowl Diary* (Lincoln, NE: University of Nebraska Press, 1984), 33.

7–8 Ibid.

  9 Toni Johnson, quoted in Deb Mulvey, editor, *We Had Everything but Money* (Greendale, WI: Reiman Publications, 1992), 31.

 10 Jeems, quoted in Federal Writers Project/Works Progress Administration, *These Are Our Lives* (Chapel Hill, NC: The University of North Carolina Press, 1939), 240.

 11 Inez Williamson, quoted in Stacey Travelstead and Jamie Reed, Oral History Project of Mooresville High School, Mooresville, Indiana, *We Made Do—Recalling the Great Depression*, April 3, 2001, <http://www.mcsc.k12.in.us/mhs/social/madedo/> (May13, 2002).

12, 13 Mr. Lee, father of Clarence, quoted in Erroll Lincoln Uys, *Teenagers on the Move during the Great Depression* (New York: TV Books, 1999), 64.

 13 Ibid., 102.

14–15 Franklin D. Roosevelt, quoted in Margaret Miner and Hugh Rawson, *American Heritage Dictionary of American Quotations* (New York: Penguin Reference, 1997), 146.

 17 Letter from a young girl, quoted in Robert Cohen, "Dear Mrs. Roosevelt: Cries for Help from Depression Youth." (*Social Education*, September 1996), 273.

 17 A journalist, quoted in Harry Swados, *American Writer and the Great Depression* (New York: Prentice Hall, 1966), 142.

23, 26 Song by Flora Robertson Shafter, quoted in Library of Congress, *Voices from the Dust Bowl: The Charles L. Todd and Robert Sonkin Migrant Worker Collection, 1940–1941*, n.d., <http://memory.loc.gov/ammem/ndlpedu/collections/vdb.index.html> (May 13, 2002).

 24 A sign in California, quoted in Mulvey, 17.

 29 A collection of letters to Eleanor Roosevelt, quoted in New Deal Network, *Dear Mrs. Roosevelt*, May 13, 2002, <http://newdeal.feri.org/eleanor/> (May 13, 2002).

 30 Ibid.

 33 Low, 15.

 34 Dorothy Simonson, quoted in Bruce Weber, editor, "What a Winter! A Teacher's Experience on Isle Royale" (*Michigan History*, May/June 1990), 31.

 38 Eleanor Roosevelt, quoted in Cohen, 270.

 38 Low, 15.

 38 A working teenager, quoted in Federal Writers Project, 233.

 39 Don Blinco, quoted in Mulvey, 152.

 40 A young girl, quoted in Katherine Dupre Lumpkin and Dorothy Wolff Douglas, *Child Workers in America* (Freeport, NY: Books for Libraries Press, 1937), 51.

 41 Blink, a hobo, quoted in Thomas Minehan, *Boy and Girl Tramps of America* (New York: Farrar and Rinehart, 1934), 204.

 42 A letter to Santa Claus, quoted in "Thick as Snowflakes, Letters Come to Central Post Office in New York City; 5,000" (New York Times, December 21, 1932), 22.

 43 Will Rogers, quoted in Donald Day, editor, *Sanity Is Where You Find It* (Cambridge, MA: Riverside Press, 1955), 137.

 44 Clancy Strock, quoted in Mulvey, 152.

 45 Mrs. Turner, mother of a sharecropping family, quoted in Federal Writers Project, 17.

 45 A letter to Santa Claus, quoted in "Thick as Snowflakes."

 48 A teenage factory worker, quoted in Federal Writers Project, 233.

 50 Blink, quoted in Minehan, 206.

 51 Franklin D. Roosevelt, quoted in Miner and Rawson.

 53 Low, 47.

 56 Ibid., 134.

SELECTED BIBLIOGRAPHY

Arnett, Hazel. *I Hear America Singing: Great Folk Songs from Revolution to Rock*. New York: Praeger Publishers, 1975.

Black, Shirley Temple. *Child Star: An Autobiography*. New York: McGraw-Hill, 1988.

Cohen, Robert. "Dear Mrs. Roosevelt: Cries for Help from Depression Youth." *Social Education*, September 1996.

Federal Writers Project/Works Progress Administration. *These Are Our Lives*. Chapel Hill, NC: The University of North Carolina Press, 1939.

Harten, Lucille Boyatt. "Depression, but Not Depressing Days." *Rendezvous*, 1984.

Kennedy, David, editor. *The American People in the Great Depression*. West Haven, CT: Pendulum Press, 1973.

Lindop, Edmund. *The Turbulent Thirties*. New York: Franklin Watts, 1970.

Lomax, Alan, Woody Guthrie, and Pete Seeger. *Hard-Hitting Songs for Hard-Hit People*. New York: Oak Publications, 1967.

Low, Ann Marie. *Dustbowl Diary*. Lincoln, NE: University of Nebraska Press, 1984.

Lumpkin, Katherine Dupre, and Dorothy Wolff Douglas. *Child Workers in America*. Freeport, NY: Books for Libraries Press, 1937.

McElvaine, Robert S. *Great Depression*. New York: Times Books, 1984.

Minehan, Thomas. *Boy and Girl Tramps of America*. New York: Farrar and Rinehart, 1934.

Moreo, Dominic W. *Schools in the Great Depression*. New York: Garland Publishing, 1996.

Morgan, Dan. *Rising in the West*. New York: Knopf, 1992.

Mulvey, Deb, editor. *We Had Everything but Money*. Greendale, WI: Reiman Publications, 1992.

Terkel, Studs. *Hard Times: An Oral History of the Great Depression*. New York: Pantheon Books, 1970.

"Thick as Snowflakes, Letters Come to Central Post Office in New York City; 5,000." *New York Times*, December 21, 1932.

Time Life Books. *The Fabulous Century: The Thirties*. New York: Time Life Books, 1969.

Weber, Bruce, editor. "What a Winter! A Teacher's Experience on Isle Royale." *Michigan History*, May/June 1990.

FURTHER READING

American Memory Learning Page. <http://memory.loc.gov/ammen/afctshtml/tshome.html>.

Coombs, Karen Mueller. *Woody Guthrie: America's Folksinger*. Minneapolis, MN: Carolrhoda Books, Inc., 2002.

Damon, Duane. *Headin' for Better Times: The Arts of the Great Depression*. Minneapolis, MN: Lerner Publications Company, 2001.

"New Deal Network: A Guide to the Great Depression of the 1930s." Franklin and Eleanor Roosevelt Institute and the Institute for Learning Technologies at Teachers College/Columbia University. <http://newdeal.feri.org/>.

Stein, Conrad. *The Great Depression*. Chicago, IL: Children's Press, 1989.

Weidt, Maryann. *Stateswoman to the World: A Story about Eleanor Roosevelt*. Minneapolis, MN: Carolrhoda Books, Inc., 1991.

Winget, Mary. *Eleanor Roosevelt*. Minneapolis, MN: Lerner Publications Company, 2001.

INDEX